HH-60 PAVE HAWK HELICOPTERS

BY DENNY VON FINN

EPIC

BELLWETHER MEDIA • MINNEAPOLIS, MN

EPIC

EPIC BOOKS are no ordinary books. They burst with intense action, high-speed heroics, and shadows of the unknown. Are you ready for an Epic adventure?

This edition first published in 2013 by Bellwether Media, Inc.

Library of Congress Cataloging-in-Publication Data

Von Finn, Denny.
HH-60 Pave Hawk helicopters / by Denny Von Finn.
p. cm. – (Epic books: military vehicles)
Includes bibliographical references and index.
Summary: "Engaging images accompany information about HH-60 Pave Hawk helicopters. The combination of high-interest subject matter and light text is intended for students in grades 2 through 7"–Provided by publisher.
ISBN 978-1-60014-819-4 (hbk. : alk. paper)
1. Pave Hawk (Search and rescue helicopter) 2. United States. Air Force–Search and rescue operations. I. Title.
UG1232.S43V66 2013
623.74'66-dc23 2012003339

Printed in the United States of America, North Mankato, MN.

A special thanks to Ted Carlson/Fotodynamics for contributing images.

TABLE OF CONTENTS

HH-60 PAVE HAWKS

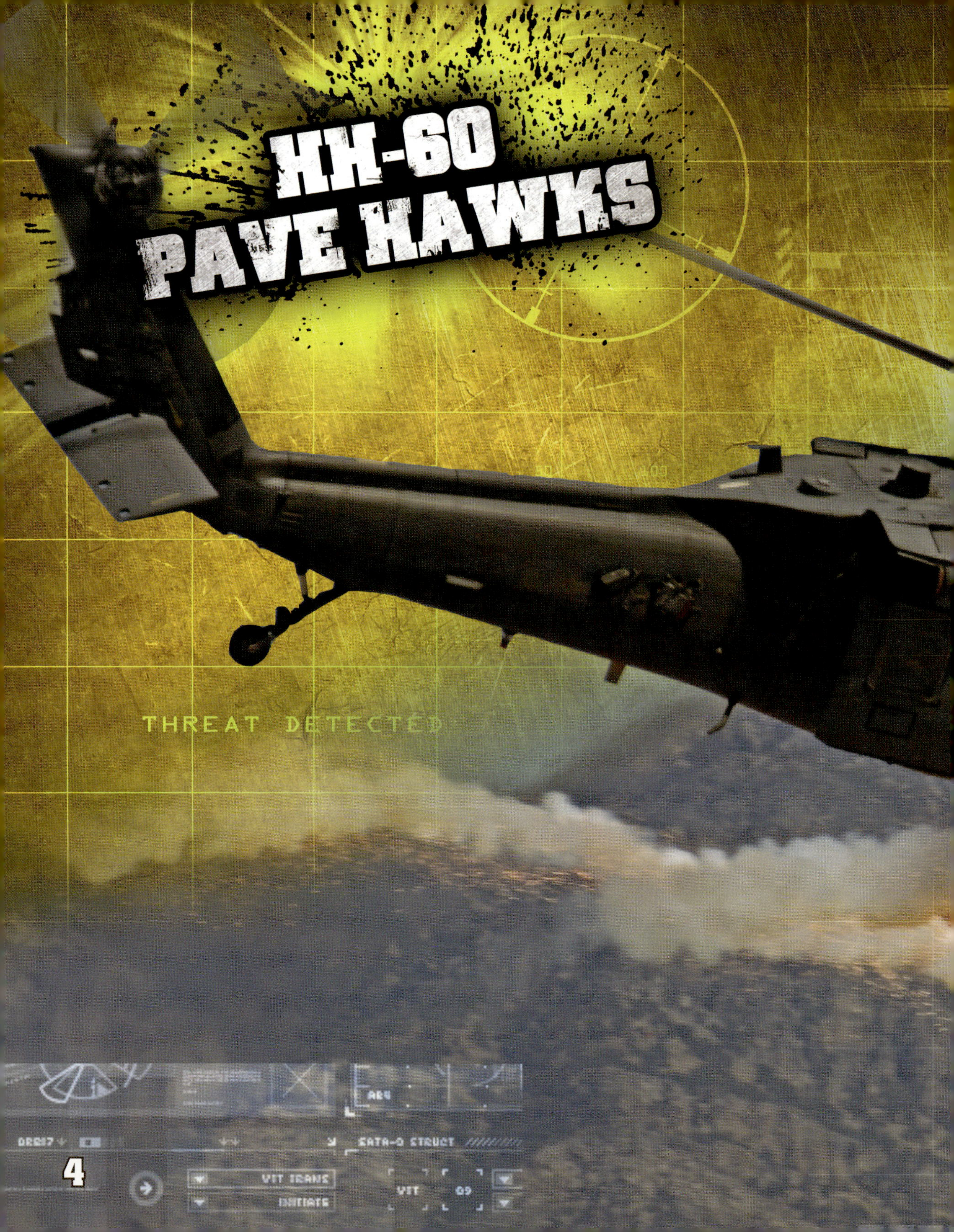

The United States Air Force sends a Pave Hawk into enemy territory. Its crew must find and rescue a **downed** pilot.

Two pilots fly the Pave Hawk. The **flight engineer** maps their **mission**. A **gunner** watches for enemies.

PILOTS

Pave Hawk Fact

The Pave Hawk is based on the design of the UH-60 Black Hawk.

The crew finds the downed pilot. They use a **hoist** to lift him into the Pave Hawk. Then the helicopter flies back to safety.

FEATURES AND WEAPONS

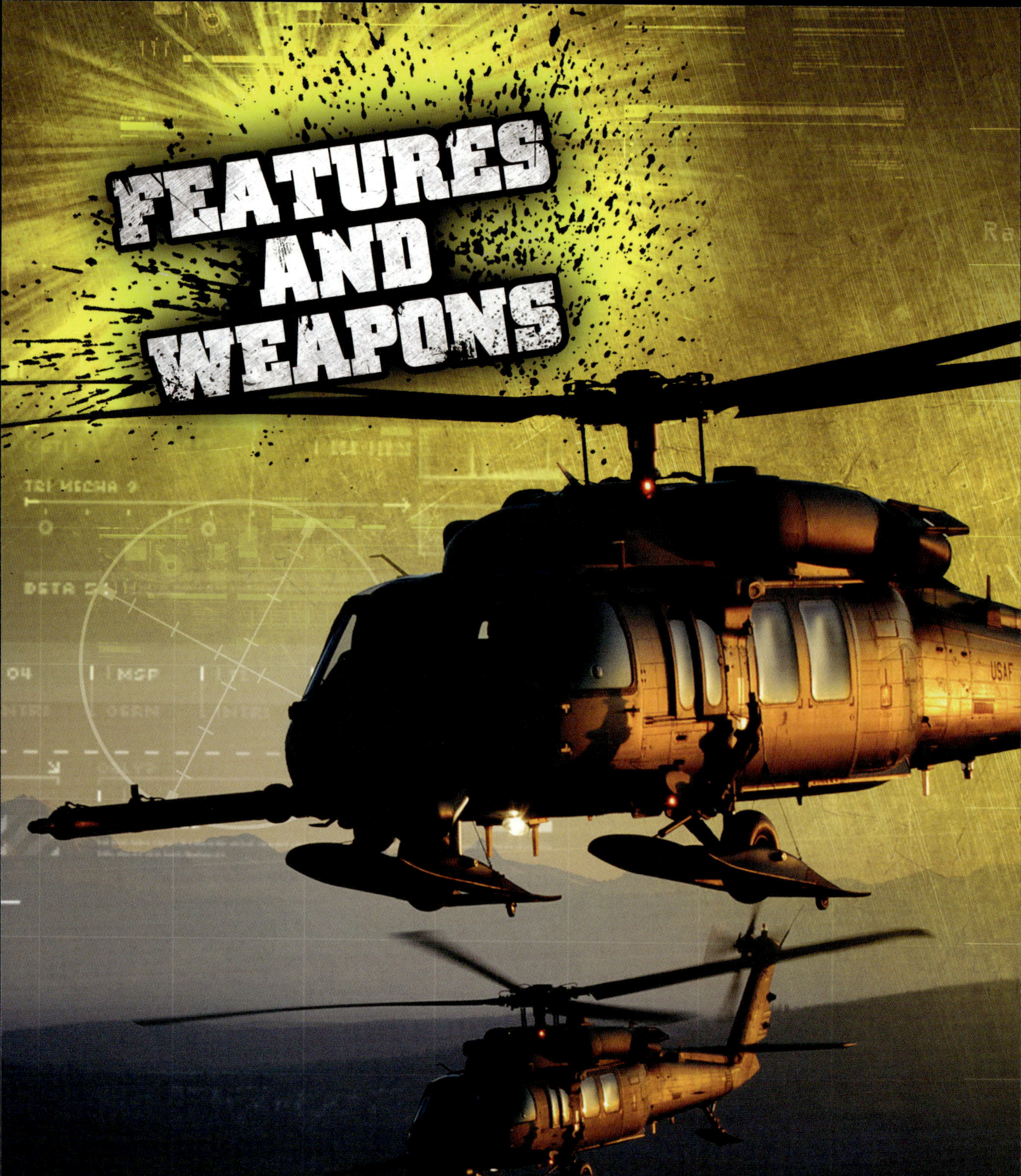

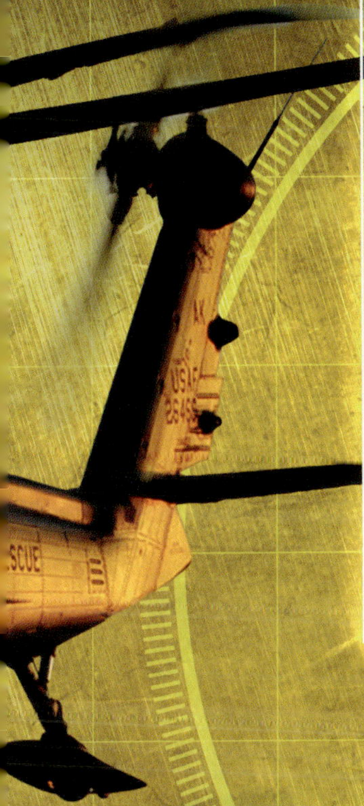

The Pave Hawk crew uses **infrared cameras** and **night-vision goggles**. These tools help them locate people and see in the dark.

The Pave Hawk's hoist has a strong cable. It is 200 feet (60 meters) long. The hoist lifts and lowers people and supplies.

Pave Hawk Fact

The Pave Hawk's hoist can lift up to 600 pounds (270 kilograms).

467
AK
USAF
26467
USAF RESCUE
LONG ISLAND

Sometimes the Pave Hawk has to fight off enemies. Two large **machine guns** are used to lay down **cover fire**.

VEHICLE BREAKDOWN: HH-60 PAVE HAWK

Used By:	U.S. Air Force
Entered Service:	1982
Length:	56.1 feet (17.1 meters)
Width:	14.4 feet (4.4 meters)
Rotor Diameter:	53.6 feet (16.3 meters)
Weight (Fully Loaded):	22,000 pounds (9,980 kilograms)
Top Speed:	184 miles (296 kilometers) per hour
Range:	580 miles (933 kilometers)
Ceiling:	14,000 feet (4,270 meters)
Crew:	4
Weapons:	two machine guns
Primary Missions:	search-and-rescue, Special Forces transport

HH-60 PAVE HAWK MISSIONS

Pave Hawks most often perform **search-and-rescue** missions. They also bring **Special Forces** into battle zones.

Level
Latitude > 44°
Longitude > 20°

Pave Hawks rescued survivors of **Hurricane Katrina** in 2005. They have also delivered food to **refugees** in Africa.

Pave Hawk Fact

Pave Hawks helped rescue more than 4,300 people after Hurricane Katrina.

Latitude > 44° 49'
Longitude > 20° 28'
Level
6195

ALASKA AIR GUARD
THREAT DETECTED

Pave Hawks have helped people in all parts of the world. These helicopters and their brave crews are always ready to lend a hand.

GLOSSARY

cover fire—shots fired to distract the enemy from their target

downed—brought to the ground

flight engineer—the crew member who operates a Pave Hawk's electronics

gunner—the crew member who uses a Pave Hawk's weapons

hoist—a giant reel used to lift people or heavy objects

Hurricane Katrina—a deadly hurricane that hit the southeastern United States in 2005; a hurricane is a spinning rainstorm that starts over warm ocean waters.

infrared cameras—cameras that detect the heat of people and objects

machine guns—automatic weapons that rapidly fire bullets

mission—a military task

night-vision goggles—goggles that let pilots see in the dark

refugees—people who flee their homeland to escape danger

search-and-rescue—a mission in which someone in a dangerous situation is brought to safety

Special Forces—troops trained to fight in small units with little support

TO LEARN MORE

At the Library

Jackson, Kay. *Military Helicopters in Action.* New York, N.Y.: PowerKids Press, 2009.

Peppas, Lynn. *Military Helicopters Flying into Battle.* New York, N.Y.: Crabtree Pub. Co., 2012.

Von Finn, Denny. *Military Helicopters.* Minneapolis, Minn.: Bellwether Media, 2010.

On the Web

Learning more about HH-60 Pave Hawks is as easy as 1, 2, 3.

1. Go to www.factsurfer.com.

2. Enter "HH-60 Pave Hawks" into the search box.

3. Click the "Surf" button and you will see a list of related Web sites.

With factsurfer.com, finding more information is just a click away.

INDEX